D0464280

Cholera

Timothy
Grayson-Jones

Cavendish
Square
New York

Published in 2015 by Cavendish Square Publishing, LLC
243 5th Avenue, Suite 136, New York, NY 10016

Website: cavendishsq.com

This publication represents the opinions and views of the author based on his or her personal
experience, knowledge, and research. The information in this book serves as a general guide only. The author
and publisher have used their best efforts in preparing this book and disclaim liability rising directly or indirectly
from the use and application of this book.

CPSIA Compliance Information: Batch #WW15CSQ

All websites were available and accurate when this book was sent to press.

Library of Congress Cataloging-in-Publication Data

Grayson-Jones, Timothy.
  Cholera / Timothy Grayson-Jones.
     pages cm. — (Deadliest diseases of all time)
  Includes bibliographical references and index.
  ISBN 978-1-50260-090-5 (hardcover) ISBN 978-1-50260-091-2 (ebook)
  1. Cholera—History—Juvenile literature. 2. Cholera—Vaccination—History—Juvenile literature. I. Title.

  RC127.G73 2015
  616.9'32—dc23

2014027325

Editor: Kristen Susienka
Senior Copy Editor: Wendy A. Reynolds
Art Director: Jeffrey Talbot
Senior Designer: Amy Greenan
Senior Production Manager: Jennifer Ryder-Talbot
Production Editor: David McNamara
Photo Researcher: J8 Media

The photographs in this book are used by permission and through the courtesy of: Cover photo and page 1, C.W. Griffin/Miami
Herald/MCT/Getty Images; Cover photo and page 1, BSIP/Universal Images Group/Getty Images; Roberto Schmidt/AFP/Getty
Images, 4; Royaltystockphoto/Science Photo Library, 8; John Snow/File:Snow-cholera-map-1.jpg/Wikimedia Commons, 14;
Rsabbatini/File:John Snow.jpg/Wikimedia Commons, 16; Chris Salvo/The Image Bank/Getty Images, 17; Thony Belizaire/AFP/
Getty Images, 20; laperla_foto/iStock/Thinkstock, 22; Hulton Archive/Getty Images, 26; Jonathan Torgovnik/Getty Images, 28;
STR/AFP/Getty Images, 29; Thony Belizaire/AFP/Getty Images, 30; © MARKA/Alamy, 33; Adam Gregor/Shutterstock.com, 35;
Print Collector/Hulton Archive/Getty Images, 36; Northfoto/Shutterstock.com, 39; Manpreet Romana/AFP/Getty Images, 42;
Justine Gerardy/AFP/Getty Images, 45; BSIP/Universal Images Group/Getty Images, 49; SABAH ARAR/AFP/Getty Images, 50;
RYO/amanaimagesRF/Getty Images, 53; Jeff Greenberg/Photolibrary/Getty Images, 55; Jonathan Torgovnik/Getty Images, 56.

Printed in the United States of America

Contents

Introduction

One of the most frightening words in medicine is **pandemic**, which is a widespread **outbreak** of an infectious disease that can cripple entire nations. One of the most famous diseases to reach pandemic level was cholera. In the past 200 years, there have been seven global cholera outbreaks. The disease can strike quickly, dehydrating a victim through overwhelming diarrhea and vomiting. If not treated immediately, patients can die from the disease in less than a day.

The first recorded cases of cholera took place in India and Britain in the early nineteenth century, but similar **epidemics** have been described for more than 2,000 years. Doctors and scientists did not know what they were dealing with until a British epidemiologist named John Snow became the first to systematically study the disease, including how it spread.

Cholera is no mystery today. Scientists and doctors have examined the disease thoroughly. They know that it's caused by a nasty bacterium—a microscopic **organism** consisting of just one tiny cell—called *Vibrio cholerae*. They also know exactly how this bacterium is spread.

A woman and her child observe a cholera alert poster in Honduras.

People usually contract cholera when they drink water or eat food that is **contaminated** with *Vibrio cholerae*. The tiny **bacteria** hitch a ride, on food or in a drink, into a person's small intestine, where digested nutrients are normally absorbed into the body. This is where the trouble starts. Within a day or two, an infection develops along the walls of the intestine. A chemical reaction takes place. Often the infection is rather tame, and the person shows no symptoms of the disease. He or she just goes on eating and drinking and living life the same way. Sometimes, however, things get bad—fast.

The first signs of cholera are a severe case of watery diarrhea and vomiting. In the worst cases, the diarrhea is so terrible it literally gushes from the body like water. In fact, it is mostly water, and therein lies the next problem: dehydration. As the victim loses body fluids, he or she becomes severely **dehydrated**. When left untreated, dehydration can be extremely dangerous. Leg muscles cramp. The skin becomes cold and droops. The circulatory system, which keeps blood flowing to all parts of the body, may collapse. Blood pressure drops. The victim may go into shock, a life-threatening condition that occurs when not enough blood makes it to the head. Kidneys and other major organs may shut down. Death is possible in just a few hours if nothing is done.

Today, of course, with the help of modern medicine and well-trained doctors, something is usually done. In fact, the disease can be treated quite easily. All a victim needs to do is stay hydrated. According to the Centers for Disease Control and Prevention (CDC), a governmental organization in the United States that combats many different diseases, fewer than 1 percent of cholera victims die if they receive the fluids they need right away.

While cholera is largely under control in the United States, it still remains a health hazard around the globe, as deadly outbreaks in Haiti in 2010 and in Iraq over the past decade indicate. In fact, much of Africa and the developing world in general still struggle with this deadly disease, despite the efforts of relief agencies around the globe. Today the World Health Organization (WHO), another recognized agency trying to eradicate or contain many diseases throughout the world, estimates that as many as 783 million people on Earth are without improved drinking water. This means that many people are at risk of developing cholera or similar painful diseases by drinking from a contaminated source.

Many men and women have attempted to understand cholera's origins and have made great strides throughout the centuries since it was first identified. However, eliminating the disease entirely continues to be a challenge. To fully comprehend cholera and its effects, and what solutions are being considered today, you must first understand what cholera is and how it develops.

one Early Cholera Outbreaks

Cholera has plagued humanity for centuries. The earliest recordings of cholera-like diseases appeared in ancient times with the writings of Hippocrates (460–377 BC), and later in those of Claudius Galen (129–216 AD), though many people suspect the illness has infected humans for much longer than that. However, while there have been indications of cholera-like diseases for thousands of years, scientists tend to label the cholera outbreak in Bengal, India, in 1817 as the first official outbreak. By that time cholera had become a familiar disease, but little was known about its origins or what caused humans to contract it. Most thought it transferred through the air, and they took precautions against catching the illness by trying a number of possible remedies—herbs, garlic, and vinegar bags. It wasn't until the 1850s that the real culprit became known. In 1817, the Bengal region, on the eastern coast of the nation, was filled with abject poverty,

Artwork of how the cholera bacteria looks close up.

and most villagers were woefully underfed. There was a lack of basic **sanitation**, which led to many residents using contaminated water and developing cholera.

Looking back, any medical professional could tell you that cholera was bound to break out in this very vulnerable population. The *Vibrio cholerae* bacterium thrives in human feces. In the unsanitary conditions of early nineteenth-century India, cholera found a welcoming home as feces made its way into the water supply, and ultimately into the guts of those who drank the water or washed their food in it.

The first cholera epidemic in India lasted for just four years. Still, thousands—perhaps even millions—died from the disease. It didn't stop there, though. After the first epidemic came to an end, new ones began. Conditions were ripe for these further outbreaks. As the sick and hungry sought help, they crowded into relief camps, towns, and cities, spreading cholera as they went. Cholera became a part of life—and a common way to die. People had no clue how to fight the disease effectively. Experts estimate that at least 15 million people died of cholera in India in the first fifty years after that initial outbreak.

Soon after the epidemics in India began, the disease began to travel around the world. Cholera became a pandemic, spreading throughout Asia, popping up in Russia, entering Europe, and eventually hitting the Americas. Millions more people died. Due to tremendous developments in worldwide trade and transportation, it was easier for people to travel from one end of the planet to the other in the nineteenth century. Wherever people traveled, cholera went with them. Contaminated food could be shipped with relative ease from an isolated village in the middle of nowhere to a major city swarming with people. Infection and disease would eventually take hold. Transportation and technology had made the planet more interconnected, but medicine and public health officials were unable to keep up with the consequences of greater globalization and the difficulties of managing large-scale outbreaks of illness.

While cholera spread around the world, the next notable epidemic hit London in 1854. A neighborhood known as Broad Street, Golden Square was overwhelmed with people dying from the disease—more than 500 people were killed by cholera in just ten days. The outbreak on Broad Street wasn't a complete surprise, but it was noteworthy for one major reason. It was there, in a neighborhood of just a few blocks, that the key to understanding cholera—what it is, what causes it, and how it can be prevented and cured—was finally discovered. This maddening and mysterious disease that had killed millions and would, over time, kill millions more, was about to be poked, prodded, examined, and, ultimately, explained. People might die, but soon, at least, they'd know why. It started with a man named John Snow.

Cholera's Diagnosis

Dr. John Snow, born in York, England on March 15, 1813, was the first person to prove that cholera could be carried in water polluted by sewage. Snow was not an epidemiologist (someone who studies diseases) by trade, but a highly respected anesthesiologist. He was one of the first doctors to use drugs such as ether and chloroform to temporarily make people unconscious or ease their pain during operations.

Snow became interested in cholera in the early 1830s as he worked on patients who were sick from the disease. Back then, no one knew for sure how cholera was spread. Most people believed it was possible to contract the disease just by breathing near someone who was already sick. The theory was that if you inhaled infected air, you stood a good chance of getting cholera.

By 1849, however, Snow had a theory of his own. During his years working on London's cholera victims, he had observed that most deaths from the disease occurred among those who got their water downstream from the city's major sewers. This led him to believe that cholera was contracted not through the air, but by swallowing water contaminated with sewage from other cholera victims. His theory was supported by the fact that most of London's drinking water was unfiltered and unsanitary.

Proof for Snow's theory finally came in the summer of 1854. It was late August, and an outbreak of cholera

Why It's Called Cholera

Many debate the origins of the word cholera. Some people think the word may have originated from the Greek word *cholēdra*, meaning "gutter"—picture rainwater gushing from a gutter following a major drenching and it's easy to imagine why. The first writer to use the word *cholera* in his writings to describe a disease was Hippocrates, and the medical writer Galen later also used this term. Although there is debate whether *cholera* referred to what we now know as cholera, the term itself has stuck and continues to define the disease today. Others suggest the name cholera derived from the word *cholās*, which means "intestine."

The true nature of the word and how it evolved into today's society may never be fully understood, but any of these suggested words address key factors in the disease's development and could be readily applied as the origin word.

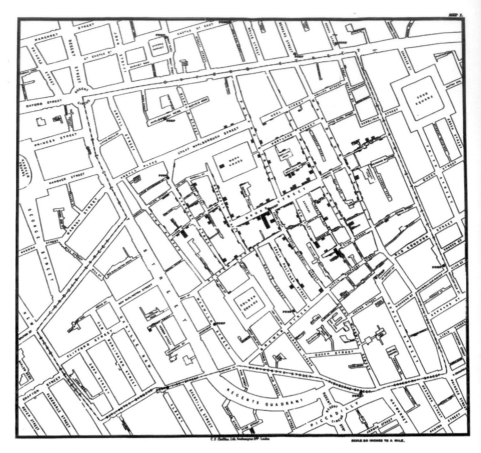

John Snow drew this map in 1854 that illustrated where
deaths in London were occurring due to cholera.

had just begun to hit a London neighborhood. Snow,
convinced that people were becoming ill because of the
water they were drinking, was determined to put an
end to the epidemic as soon as possible. Hundreds of
people were dying. Thousands more were at risk.

To pinpoint the source of the disease, Snow used a
map of the area to plot points showing exactly where
each person had died. He also noted the source of the

neighborhood's water supply, a pump on Broad Street. Looking at his map, the answer was obvious. Most of the deaths up until that point were clustered within a few hundred yards of the water pump. The people who were dying were the same people who drew their water from the Broad Street pump. Certain he had found the source of the outbreak, Snow went to the pump himself and took a look at the water. Even without a microscope, he could see that the water was filthy. He knew he had found the culprit.

Today, **mapping** incidents of diseases—or "**medical geography**"—as it's now known, is used all the time by scientists, doctors, and other medical professionals as they strive to learn more about how diseases such as cholera move within a population. Of course, modern-day researchers have much more sophisticated techniques at their disposal than Snow did, who probably did everything by hand. Thanks to computers, special software programs, satellites, and other high-tech gadgets, mapping is now a highly specialized science.

On September 7, 1854, Snow presented his research to the local authorities and asked them to remove the pump's handle to prevent more people from drinking the water. The next day the handle was taken away, and the epidemic was stopped cold in its tracks. Thousands of lives were saved.

The following year, Snow published a book titled *On the Mode of Communication of Cholera.*

A Closer History

1817 First reported cholera epidemic takes place in India.

John Snow.

Early 1830s John Snow begins studying cholera by working with patients who are infected with the disease.

1849 Snow develops theory that cholera is a water-borne disease.

1849 Cholera outbreak takes place in Chicago and 678 people die.

1854 Cholera breaks out in London, England.

1854 In London, Snow presents and tests theory about cholera being a water-borne disease. Tests are a success.

1947 Cholera breaks out in Egypt.

1961 Worldwide cholera pandemic begins on Indonesian island of Celebes.

1963 Pandemic hits Bangladesh.

1964 Pandemic hits India.

1965 Pandemic hits the Soviet Union.

Some workers on oil rigs have contracted cholera by eating marine life from polluted waters.

1970 Pandemic hits South Africa.

1973 Pandemic hits Europe.

1981 Seventeen people contract cholera on an oil rig off the coast of Texas.

1991 Pandemic hits South America.

1991 Eight cases of cholera reported in New Jersey.

1992 New strain of cholera breaks out in India and Bangladesh.

2007 First of several cholera outbreaks hits postwar Iraq.

2010 Months after a deadly earthquake rocks Haiti, a cholera outbreak kills more than 8,000. It is later determined that the disease was introduced by United Nations peacekeepers.

In the book he explained his theory that cholera was a water-borne disease. Still, despite the proof that Snow found on Broad Street, it took many years for the rest of the world to accept his views. However, Snow is now recognized as one of the first people to ever use meticulous observation and maps to understand how a disease is spread. **Epidemiology** owes much to Snow, as do the people whose lives his research has helped save.

The Seventh Pandemic

For the rest of the nineteenth century, pandemics of cholera came and went in waves. Just when people thought the disease had disappeared for good, it would appear again. All told, there were six pandemics between the first outbreak in 1817 and the end of the century. Then, in the first half of the twentieth century, the disease seemed to rest. It was still present in Asia, but aside from a devastating epidemic in Egypt in 1947, it didn't appear in epidemic proportions anywhere else in the world. Then, in 1961, the world's seventh cholera pandemic kicked in. It was born as an epidemic on the Indonesian island of Celebes and began to spread. Known as *Vibrio cholerae* 01, biotype El Tor, it hit Bangladesh in 1963, India a year later, and the Soviet Union, Iran, and Iraq the year after that. By 1970, El Tor had hit West Africa, a region that hadn't seen cholera for at least a century. From there, the disease marched east to engulf the entire African continent.

In 1973, the cholera pandemic spread to Europe. It hit Japan and the South Pacific later in the decade. Still, for those in the Western Hemisphere, including people living in North, South, and Central America, the disease was still relatively unknown. For example, South America hadn't had a cholera outbreak all century.

Good luck never lasts forever, of course, and in January 1991, cholera swept ashore on the banks of South America. Peru was the first country to be hit. From there, it spread quickly. Within two years, more than 50 percent of all cholera cases were occurring in the Western Hemisphere. By 1994, almost a million cases of cholera caused by the El Tor biotype had been reported to the World Health Organization by twenty-one Western countries.

Cholera remains a deadly disease today. Health care organizations estimate that the disease affects three to five million people every year, and that it claims the lives of more than 100,000 annually. A number of relief organizations are doing what they can to decrease the numbers, including distributing **vaccines** and working to improve local sanitation and medical facilities. However, it does not appear that cholera will be conquered any time soon.

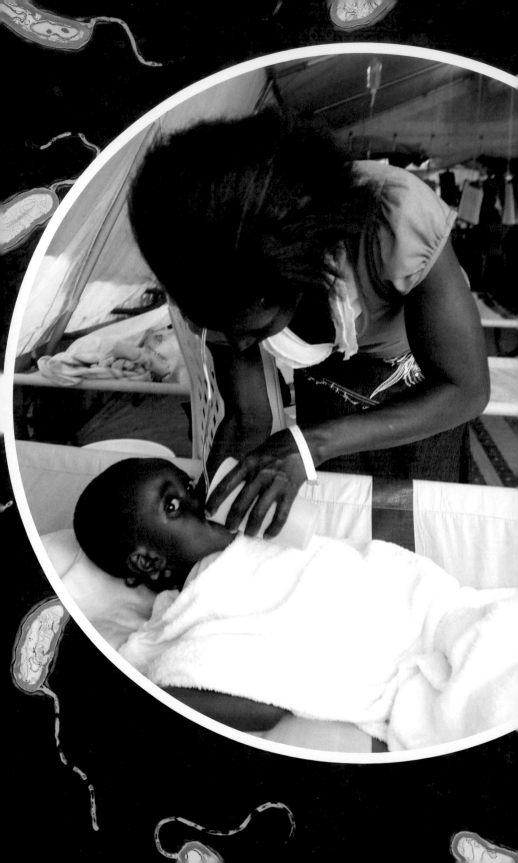

two Waves of Cholera

While the infamous 1817 India and 1854 London outbreaks of cholera are the two most remembered in the history books, there were still numerous incidents of cholera all over the globe. Most were not on such a massive scale—often the disease would only affect an isolated group of individuals. Also, cholera is not always deadly—sometimes the doctor treating the individual would not even realize it was cholera. However, cholera still remained a significant health hazard throughout the nineteenth and twentieth centuries.

Here in the United States, cholera has had a very short and relatively quiet history. It pops up once in a while, but never to the extent that it's seen in Africa, Asia, and Latin America. Thanks to well-developed waste-treatment systems and good **sanitary** conditions in most parts of the United States, cholera almost never has the opportunity to infect

Cholera has been around for a long time but is relatively easy to combat with good sanitation and staying hydrated.

Crabmeat and other seafood can be infected with the cholera bacteria. Be careful when you eat seafood, especially in places that do not have good sanitation or fresh drinking water.

people. Most U.S.-based cases of cholera are contracted abroad and then brought back to the United States.

Still, when cholera does appear, it definitely turns heads. Such was the case in 1991 in New Jersey. Between March 31 and April 3 of that year, eight residents of the state became ill after eating crabmeat flown in from Ecuador, a country in South America. One of the victims had bought the meat at an Ecuadorian fish market, carried it home on a plane, and served it in a salad to family and friends. Within days of the meal, everyone who ate the meat came down with watery diarrhea. Five of the people experienced vomiting, and three had terrible leg cramps. Five people wound up in the hospital. Doctors who treated the victims examined their stools and found half of them to be contaminated with the El Tor variety of *Vibrio cholerae* 01, the same serotype, or strain, responsible for the January epidemic in South America. Fortunately for all those involved, and thanks to prompt treatment with modern medicine, no one died.

The outbreak in New Jersey wasn't the first time this century that cholera hit the United States. In fact, El Tor had popped up around the country every once in a while for almost twenty years. For example, in 1973 one person contracted cholera in Texas. No one knows why. Five years later, there were eight more cases in Louisiana. Later, in 1981, seventeen people came down with the disease while working on a floating oil rig off the coast of Texas. Scientists don't think these cases had anything to do with poor sanitation. Rather, they believe the cholera was contracted when the victims ate shellfish from coastal waters where the *Vibrio cholerae* bacteria thrive. They believe the shellfish were contaminated with cholera and that by eating this fish the people became sick.

Since the 1970s, cholera cases continue to be reported in the United States. Relative to countries in other parts of the world, however, the cases are rare and usually minor. On average, the CDC reports there are six cases of cholera contracted in the United States each year. The most recent outbreak occurred in 2010 when American families visiting Hispaniola (Haiti and the Dominican Republic) contracted the disease and brought it back to the United States. Between 2010 and 2011, there were twenty-three cases reported in the United States—almost all patients had travelled to Hispaniola to visit relatives or for a vacation.

Cholera continues to affect countries around the world. Latin American and African countries have the world's highest cholera rates. As long as poor sanitation exists, cholera will continue. However, if sewage and water treatment systems are brought up to standard, future cholera outbreaks will become far less likely. Although cholera may be easy to prevent, all it takes to contract it is forgetting to wash a contaminated fruit or vegetable, or drinking water that is contaminated.

Chicago's Cholera History

Long before current treatment methods were established, or even the cause of such a disease was fully understood, cholera affected parts of the United States. It had been brought over by European immigrants in the 1830s, and first entered the United States via Canada. It impacted populations in New York City, Detroit, and Buffalo. However, perhaps the hardest-hit area was Chicago in the mid-nineteenth century.

Cholera hit Chicago several times in the 1800s. Experts believe the city's first bout with the disease was in 1832. It is suspected that infected soldiers transferred the

Cholera Hospitals

When cholera ravaged the streets of U.S. cities in 1832, many physicians and boards of health advised keeping the infected patient indoors, away from people. This method of seclusion is called a quarantine, and it has been enacted for many other illnesses in the past.

Another area hit hard during the summer of 1832 was New York. New York City established a board of health in 1822, when an epidemic of yellow fever hit. In 1832, when the cholera epidemic erupted, it became clear that the usual methods of treating diseases would not work. Once enough people had suffered or died from the disease, New York City health officials recommended building cholera hospitals. They built five hospitals around the city, in the hope of treating as many people as possible. These hospitals specifically catered to the needs of ill patients, though not everyone was happy to send their relatives there. Conditions at the time were rumored to be less than safe. Whether the hospitals did any good is up for debate; however, by Christmas of 1832, cases of cholera within the city had disappeared.

Chicago (pictured here in 1860) was affected by multiple cholera pandemics throughout the nineteenth century.

disease from Buffalo, New York. The soldiers had gone to Illinois to meet Black Hawk, a Native American leader, and his troops. The Native Americans had returned to the area after being exiled in 1831, and armies from all over the United States had been called to remove them. The infected Buffalo soldiers brought cholera into the city. That year was devastating to Chicago—out of a population of thousands, hundreds of people died.

Action to combat the threat was taken quickly. In 1834, the city of Chicago set up its first board of health, which was a relatively new concept at that time. In the following years, as people learned more about the disease, Chicago did a number of things to improve the quality of its drinking water and sewage systems. By the 1870s, cholera was no longer a problem.

Below is a list of the cholera epidemics that followed the outbreak of 1832.

Year	Deaths in Chicago
1849	678
1850	420
1851	216
1852	630
1853	1
1854	1,424
1855	147
1856–1865	Not significant
1866	990
1867	10

The threat of this and other diseases would continue to affect the city. However, with each new epidemic, new opportunities to prepare for its effects were taken. For example, these outbreaks led to the creation of cemeteries, orphanages, and Chicago's first hospitals.

A New Strain

Until relatively recently, *Vibrio cholerae* 01 was the only serotype, or strain, of the bacteria known to cause epidemic cholera. Other serotypes were well known to scientists, but they never caused more than basic diarrhea, and certainly never led to anything of epidemic proportions.

A second serogroup of *Vibrio cholerae* 01, known as *Vibrio cholerae* O139, was identified in 1992 in Bangladesh. This strain was capable of causing

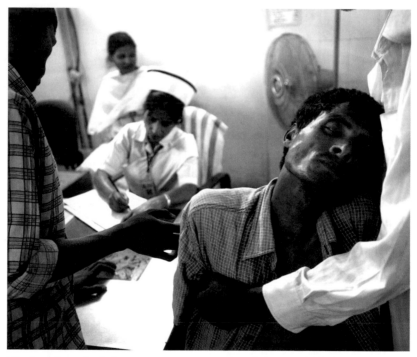

Cholera hospitals have been set up around the world to help treat ill patients.

A Chinese health worker disinfects a classroom in an area affected by a cholera outbreak in 2010.

outbreaks as well. *Vibrio cholerae* O139 is currently confined to Southeast Asia, but in the past, cholera has been capable of expanding beyond its borders.

Recently, scientists have identified new variant strains in both Asia and Africa. They continue to monitor these strains to see whether the number of epidemic-causing serotypes has further increased.

The Science three Behind Cholera

S cientists and researchers have been studying cholera for more than a century and a half, and in that time they've managed to learn much about how the disease works, including where the bacteria thrives (contaminated water and food), how it enters the human body, and how it passes from host to host. In areas of the world with poor sanitation, the bacteria are far more likely to cause an outbreak. Scientists also now know how the virus can move from one part of the globe to another. A human host who is infected in an area where the bacteria is present can act as a carrier, bringing cholera to a new region. An example of this occurred in 2010 in Haiti. After an earthquake struck early that year, an outbreak of cholera hit the island. What was unusual was that cholera was not indigenous, or native, to the island. It seemed that something else was responsible for bringing it there.

People carry medical kits to aid in preventing cholera in Haiti.

When investigating the cause of the outbreak, medical investigators believed a sewage leak in a United Nations base resulted in a river being infected with cholera. Ironically, people who had come to help the island ravaged by a natural disaster had introduced a further problem to the country.

In addition, climate change has also been identified as a trigger to the spread of cholera. Some scientists have noted that a cholera outbreak in Latin America in 1991 may have been due at least in part to the warmer temperatures caused by El Niño weather patterns, which could have created the warm conditions that are ideal for the cholera bacteria. Another factor in the disease's emergence in South America for the first time in decades may have been increased international trade and the ease with which goods (and any **microbes** they may be carrying) are now shipped throughout the world. It is quite easy for food contaminated with cholera to travel from one end of the world to the other. Finally, Peru had recently reduced certain measures it normally used to ensure that its water supply was pure and bacteria-free, such as treatment with chlorine. This may have also aided the emergence of the disease.

How did people figure out the disease was caused by bacteria? To answer that question, we must understand the work of not only John Snow, but also men named Filippo Pacini and Robert Koch. They also had a great effect on the history of cholera and science's understanding of it.

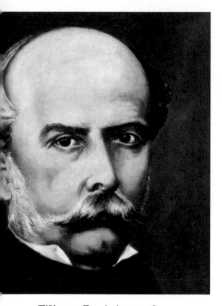

Filippo Pacini was the first person to prove John Snow's germ theory correct, unknown to Snow.

Filippo Pacini and Cholera

The same year John Snow published his findings about the Broad Street pump experiment and the cause of cholera, his theory, called germ theory, was proven correct—unbeknownst to him and much of the world. The man to do so was Filippo Pacini. Born in Pistoia, Italy in 1812, Pacini joined the medical profession at the age of twenty-eight. While in medical school, he discovered oval objects attached to nerves, which are now known as Pacinian corpuscles. In 1854, he became the first person to identify with a microscope the bacterium that caused cholera. Pacini published a paper about his discovery, but it was completely ignored by the scientists of the time. It is unlikely that Snow or the next man to confirm the cholera bacterium's existence, Robert Koch, knew about him or his paper. However, in 1965, eighty years after Pacini's death, he finally became recognized

Testing the Water

Where do you get your drinking water? From a lake? From a stream? From a private well deep beneath the ground? Or do you drink only bottled water? Depending on where you live, you probably drink water that comes from one or more of these sources.

Do you have any idea what that water contains?

Probably not. To be honest, your water is, most likely, perfectly safe to drink. Thanks to the Clean Water Act, which was passed into law by the U.S. Congress in 1972, polluted waterways are relatively rare. Cities are now required to maintain wastewater treatment plants that keep polluted water from entering our drinking water supplies. States are also required to adhere to strict water quality standards. Tap water rules prohibit contamination with bacteria like E. coli or fecal coliform, which would be present if the water contained fecal matter. In big cities that use surface waters, such as rivers, lakes, or streams, for their drinking water supply, the Environmental Protection Agency (EPA) requires the use of filtering or disinfectants to prevent contamination of water with cholera bacteria.

In the United States, the likelihood of contracting a disease such as cholera by drinking tap water is extremely slim.

Still, it never hurts to keep tabs on your water. In the same way you

would examine the list of ingredients on a box of cereal, it's a good idea to see exactly what's in the water that pours from your tap.

For more information on drinking water safety, water pollution, ocean waters, and water conservation, among other issues, visit the Natural Resources Defense Council's website, nrdc.org. For a list of laboratories certified by your state to test drinking water, as well as basic information about drinking water and the EPA's drinking water program, visit water.epa.gov/drink.

Alternatively, look up your local, county, or state health departments online. Some local health departments test private water, such as well water, for free. Finally, if you're interested in filtering your tap water yourself, be sure to purchase a filter that is certified by the National Sanitation Foundation.

for his contribution to the medical field. Cholera is now officially known in the medical profession as *Vibrio cholera Pacini 1854*.

Once the culprit of cholera was discovered, the next step involved the work of Louis Pasteur, who was able to prove through chemical experiments that germs could and did cause illnesses.

The Work of Robert Koch

Robert Koch is known for his studies of the cholera bacteria.

Robert Koch, a scientist born in Clausthal, Germany, in 1843, followed in Pacini's footsteps, although unknowingly. As one of the founders of the science of bacteriology (the study of bacteria), he also showed that specific **microorganisms**, or bacteria, cause specific diseases.

Working in the late 1800s, at a time when cholera was one of the most feared and deadly diseases in the world, Koch spent many long hours in his laboratory and traveled the world. He had a problem, though. While he and other scientists had an idea that microscopic organisms were behind diseases such as cholera, many people questioned their existence entirely. These creatures were impossible to see, even through a microscope.

Koch came up with a solution. He found a way to stain the microbes with dye. The dye allowed him to photograph the microbes under a microscope and study them more effectively. Using this technique, he was able to identify the microbes that cause tuberculosis in 1882. A year later, in 1883, he determined exactly which bacteria cause cholera. He then confirmed Snow's original suspicion that the cholera organism can be carried in water and on food.

Koch's work, which included trips to Egypt and India, where cholera was rampant, eventually led to proof that pollution by certain bacteria spread disease. Water polluted with cholera bacteria, for example, spread cholera to those who drank it. His research also showed that the cholera bacteria could spread from population to population through the diarrhea of its victims. By the turn of the century, Koch and his assistants had used the microbe-dyeing method to identify more than twenty specific germs that cause disease. Unlike Pacini, the first man to investigate this, Koch's results were accepted by the scientific community, for which he won the Nobel Prize for Physiology and Medicine in 1905.

Other countries have been stricken by cholera thanks to the migration of people. For example, war forces people to flee their homes. Sometimes they end up crowded into refugee camps, where conditions are unsanitary and limited medical supplies are devoted to many problems other than cholera. Economic conditions can also play a part. Poor people from small villages where cholera is endemic may move to cities to look for work and end up bringing the disease with them.

Despite the fact that doctors and other medical experts are well aware of how to prevent cholera outbreaks and how to treat them when they do occur, cholera continues to be a major threat to public health in many parts of the world. When established medical facilities are removed or understaffed, or when cholera strikes a region of the world where such facilities never existed, the disease becomes dangerous and has the potential to kill many people. Even in the industrialized world, where diseases of epidemic proportions don't often strike, cholera can break out in cities where water purification is not adequate or has been disabled. All over the world, cholera appears in places where public health measures have broken down and reliable water supplies no longer exist.

Tracking the Spread of Cholera

Since the days of London's Broad Street epidemic in the mid-1800s, technology has changed tremendously. Modern day scientists now use a number of disciplines, including ecology, oceanography, microbiology, marine biology, and epidemiology, to predict when cholera

Cholera can spread among people, especially in refugee camps set up for residents of war-torn areas.

epidemics are likely to occur. It's even possible to track *Vibrio cholerae* with special space-based satellite imaging equipment designed to follow the movements of ocean organisms on which the bacteria often live. By determining when these marine organisms (and their hitchhiking *Vibrio cholerae* partners) are going to hit shore, scientists can predict when a coastal area is most vulnerable to a cholera outbreak and can warn people to take extra care with their food and water. The technology also gives medical professionals and aid workers time to prepare medicine and facilities for an epidemic before it takes place.

Global Warming and Cholera

Most scientists agree that the world is getting warmer. In recent years, studies have shown that temperatures around the planet are on the rise. In fact, according to the National Oceanic and Atmospheric Administration, 2013 was the fourth warmest year ever recorded (2010 was the warmest), and it was the thirty-seventh consecutive year that the global temperature was above average. The trend continues, and things are only getting hotter. The WHO estimates that the average temperature of Earth's surface will rise by 1.5 to 3.5 degrees Celsius (2.7 to 6.3 degrees Fahrenheit) by 2100.

If you like to go to the beach, this may come as good news, but global warming, as it's called, is not so simple. As Earth warms up, other environmental changes—some good, some bad—are likely to take place as well.

One environmental change that may take place thanks to global warming is a worldwide rise in the sea level. The WHO predicts that the sea level will rise by 15 to 95 centimeters (6 to 37 inches) in the next 100 years. Why? One of the main reasons is something known as thermal expansion. As the oceans warm up, physical processes cause them to expand, or get bigger.

What does this mean for cholera? It's hard to know for sure, but some scientists believe that as the world's temperatures and sea levels rise, so will cholera outbreaks. One theory suggests that changes in ocean currents that result from thermal expansion will lead to upwellings along shorelines. Upwellings occur when an unusual amount of nutrient-rich waters, normally found near the ocean bottom, rise to the surface. For microscopic plants known as **phytoplankton**, which float on the surface, drift with the currents, and thrive on such nutrients, upwellings mean feast time. Before long, the phytoplankton population explodes.

This population explosion triggers an interesting chain of events. When phytoplankton numbers increase, the typical result is a rise in phytoplankton-eating animals called **zooplankton**. Scientists have shown that cholera bacteria can live and multiply in the guts of certain kinds of zooplankton. In fact, one team of scientists believes that an increase in the zooplankton population may have been partially to blame for the 1991 cholera epidemic in Latin America that killed thousands of people.

The tie of global warming and an increase in cholera is the subject of much debate, with a recent study published in 2011 in the *American Journal of Tropical Medicine and Hygiene* looking to debunk the claims. Whether or not global warming is a trigger of additional cases, all scientists and researchers agree that finding an effective vaccine, improving public health throughout the world, and eliminating the unsanitary conditions that allow cholera to thrive are crucial to bringing down the number of global cases of cholera.

Preventing and Combating Cholera

Thanks to everything scientists and medical researchers have learned about cholera in the last hundred years, our ability to curb and cure the disease has increased significantly. Now that health officials know how the disease spreads, they are focusing efforts to improve sanitation throughout the developing world in order to prevent outbreaks from even happening. Another effective method for curbing cholera is education, since people armed with knowledge are far more likely to make safe choices with water and food and avoid the bacteria altogether.

Avoiding Cholera

Although cholera outbreaks continue to occur around the world, the chances of your contracting the disease are extremely low. In fact, according to the Centers for Disease Control and Prevention, even if you're traveling in an area where cholera is common, your chances of getting the disease are about one in a million.

A man sits in front of cholera awareness posters.

43

Although the odds are in your favor, if you're traveling in an area with epidemic cholera, it is still wise to follow a few basic rules to ensure your health. The following is a list of things the World Health Organization recommends that you do (and don't do) when you're in a region where cholera may be present.

1. Drink only water that has been boiled or disinfected with chlorine, iodine, or other suitable products. Products for disinfecting water are generally available in pharmacies. Beverages such as hot tea or coffee, wine, beer, carbonated water or soft drinks, and bottled or packaged fruit juices are also usually safe to drink.

2. Wash your hands regularly with soap and safe water. If you do not have soap nearby, you can scrub your hands with ash or sand. Always rinse with safe water.

3. Eat food that has been thoroughly cooked and is still hot when served. Cooked food that has been held at room temperature for several hours and served without being reheated can be a major source of infection.

4. Avoid raw seafood and other raw food, except fruits and vegetables that you have peeled or shelled yourself. Remember this simple rule: Cook it, peel it, or leave it.

5. Never use any body of water as a toilet.

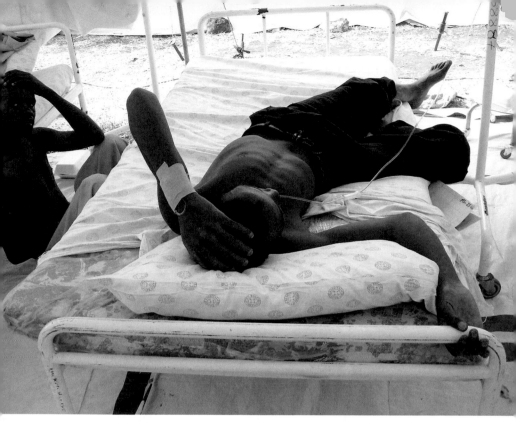

To help people recover from cholera, rehydration tents are set up in cholera-affected areas.

What to Do If You Get Cholera

Despite everything that can be done to avoid the disease, cholera still manages to strike many populations and kill thousands of people every year. Fortunately for those who do contract cholera, there are several things that can be done to keep the disease from becoming deadly.

The preferred method of treatment is very simple and usually successful. Since cholera victims die because of dehydration and complications that result from dehydration, the best thing to do is replace the fluids and salts lost through diarrhea and vomiting. Major aid organizations treat patients with a specially formulated oral rehydration solution, a pre-packaged mix of sugar and salts that can be combined with water for easy drinking. This works almost 90 percent of the time. In exceptionally severe cases, however, when the patient is on the verge of death or is not able to drink the solution, doctors must force the fluids into the patient's body intravenously. In either case, less than one percent of patients die if they're able to **rehydrate** right away. On the other hand, **case-fatality rates** are as high as 50 percent when no treatment is available. This usually occurs in communities that are not prepared for a cholera epidemic and where there are no available facilities for treatment.

Vacationing Abroad

If you or your family are planning a trip to a country where cholera may be present, it's a good idea to do a little research before you go. Two organizations—the CDC and the WHO—are great resources for cholera-related information. For up-to-date news on the latest outbreaks around the world, visit the Centers for Disease Control and Prevention's cholera website, cdc.gov/cholera/index.html. It has an interactive map that allows you to click on individual countries in order to learn more about their current status. The World

The Safety of Imported Food

Food and water imported to other countries go through many safety checks before being transported around the world. According to the WHO, "at present [there is] no information that food commercially imported from affected countries has been implicated in outbreaks of cholera in importing countries." Many of the cases of cholera entering the United States or other countries has been the result of individual travelers bringing contaminated food or drink back and giving it to family or friends. "Therefore," says the WHO, "it may be concluded that food produced under good manufacturing practices poses only a negligible risk for cholera transmission." Be aware when you travel of just where you are and what sorts of foods and liquids you eat or drink. You never know where cholera might be lurking.

Health Organization's website also includes current information regarding cholera around the world: who.int/topics/cholera/en.

Some cholera patients are given **antibiotics** during the early stages of the illness. Effective antibiotics can help reduce the amount of diarrhea the victim has and the amount of fluids required for rehydration. For the patient, that's good news. The problem with antibiotics, however, is they don't do anything to stem the spread of cholera.

Developing an Effective Vaccine

Researchers have developed both oral and injectable vaccines for cholera, but they're not particularly effective because they only provide protection from the disease for a short while. The vaccine is made of dead *Vibrio cholerae* bacteria. The World Health Organization does not recommend it to travelers or to countries hoping to prevent the disease from crossing their borders. The WHO feels that vaccinations may give people a false sense of security and lead them to disregard other cholera-fighting measures that are much more permanent and effective, such as stopping the disease at its source—usually the water supply. Likewise, international health regulations do not require any traveler to be vaccinated against the disease. This may change in the future, of course, as better, more permanent vaccines are developed. The Maryland-based National Institute of Allergy and

Scientists today are inventing new ways of controlling and eliminating cholera from the world.

Infectious Diseases (NIAID), a division of the U.S. government's National Institutes of Health (NIH), is currently testing new vaccines and new ways to treat cholera and other diarrheal diseases.

A new single-dose vaccine is in the process of being developed. The company, PaxVax Inc., calls the oral vaccine PXVX 0200, and they plan to submit the product to the Food and Drug Administration (FDA) for approval in 2015. What makes the vaccine so encouraging is that travelers would only need to take a single dose, whereas the current vaccines need two doses to be effective.

five Continuing the Fight Against Cholera

ith the continued development of vaccines and the improvement of sanitation around the world, organizations such as the WHO and the CDC continue their work to eradicate the causes of cholera. They've got their work cut out for them, as seemingly unrelated events like the war in Iraq or the earthquake in Haiti can create new conditions that spur cholera outbreaks. Public health officials are attempting to get better at predicting when cholera will strike in order to better equip populations with information on how to prevent cholera as well as how to treat it if they do get the disease.

Preventing Cholera Through Foods

As science advances, there are other ways to possibly prevent the spread of cholera. Scientists around the

Children gather around a pump bringing fresh water to their village.

world are working to create edible vaccines through a process called genetic engineering. This does not mean that you can eat a certain food and receive immunity from a disease. Rather, there are steps to introduce vaccination by using certain foods to store it and putting those foods into medicine tablets, so that a person, one day, can consume the right dosage. The potato was one of the first foods scientists experimented on to create an edible vaccine in 1998. At the time, using genetic engineering was a relatively new concept. However, it is becoming more common in the medical field. In 2007, a Japanese research team revealed they had successfully developed a cholera vaccine in rice through genetic engineering. This rice had been tested on mice and had positive results, but the reality of an edible rice vaccine becoming available to humans is still a long way off.

The idea of genetic engineering is surprisingly simple: Take a microscopic sample of the cholera toxin and, using sophisticated laboratory techniques, insert it into food. Later, as the food with this new gene grows, a tiny, safe-to-eat amount of the cholera toxin is present in every one of its cells. When a doctor then gives a bite-sized piece of the special food to a patient to eat, the food acts exactly like a vaccination shot designed to increase the body's ability to protect against disease. As the food is digested, the cholera toxin sticks like glue to cells in the patient's gut and causes the production of

Rice is one of the foods being genetically engineered to hold an oral cholera vaccine.

antibodies, which fight like fearless soldiers to destroy the toxin. Then, even after the toxin is defeated, the antibodies remain for months or even years, ready to do battle again if the need should arise. Should the patient run into real cholera during that time, whether because he or she drinks contaminated water or eats contaminated food, he or she is protected and won't get sick.

As great as this concept might seem, there are potential drawbacks to genetically engineered food. The main issue is that the environmental hazards of introducing strange genes into ordinary food are slowly becoming known but have not been fully understood. Another concern is food, such as potatoes, that might need to be heated. Heat may make the medicine useless. However, if the medical professionals responsible for these breakthroughs present the vaccine in a more digestible format, such as a powdered capsule, the food would maintain its immunological efficiencies.

A Growing World Leads to Growing Epidemics

As the world's population grows, certain areas are becoming more and more crowded, and diseases are becoming more and more common. Consider these statistics on population growth and ask yourself these difficult questions: If the world's population continues to rise, yet the planet Earth remains the same size, where is everybody going to go? How will they avoid the spread of deadly diseases?

- Worldwide, about 2.5 billion people were alive in 1950.
- More than 7 billion people were alive in 2014.
- According to the U.S. Census Bureau, at the current rate of growth, the world population will hit 9 billion by 2044.
- The population of India is expected to reach more than 1.53 billion by 2030.
- The population of Bangladesh is expected to hit 196.6 million by 2030.
- There were 318.4 million people living in the United States in 2014.

By increasing sanitation in impoverished areas, cholera can be defeated.

- The population of the United States will hit 358.5 million by 2030.*

For now, residents of the United States face very little risk of contracting cholera, whether here at home or while traveling abroad. As health workers fight the disease in other parts of the world, the risk should decrease even further. Still, that doesn't mean cholera is no longer a threat. Many poor and developing countries need the medical assistance and training

* All figures from the United States Census Bureau, census.gov

Medical advancements can one day eliminate cholera from all areas of the world.

which nations such as the United States can provide. Fortunately, as medical professionals conduct more research and learn more about diseases like cholera, they can better help the areas that need it most and develop more effective strategies of prevention.

Despite the hard work of medical researchers and relief organizations, cholera continues to be a problem, particularly in Africa and Southeast Asia. Attempts to find a vaccine continue, but many believe that repairing the economies of the developing world, particularly in the areas of housing, sanitation, and water delivery and storage, are the true keys to eradicating cholera. Eliminating poverty will be a significant step in ridding the world of cholera, but it's likely that this deadly disease will stay with us for some time.

Glossary

antibiotic A substance made by scientists, and given to infected patients, that kills or stops the growth of microorganisms that cause disease.

bacteria Single-celled microscopic organisms that sometimes cause disease in humans, animals, or plants, but are often harmless or beneficial to life. The singular form is bacterium.

case-fatality rate The proportion of people with a particular disease who die because of it. For example, a case-fatality rate of 20 percent means that twenty out of every 100 people who acquired the disease died.

contaminate To make impure or unclean.

dehydrate To lose more body fluids than normal, whether because of vomiting, diarrhea, or other bodily problems. Severe dehydration can lead to death if left untreated.

epidemic Also known as an "outbreak." The sudden increase in occurrence of a particular disease in a community or population.

Glossary

epidemiology A branch of medical science that examines and tracks how diseases occur in populations.

mapping The scientific method of mapping out where people are who come down with a particular disease in an effort to understand how that disease spreads. Also called medical geography.

medical geography The scientific method of mapping out where people are who come down with a particular disease in an effort to understand how that disease spreads. Also called mapping.

microbe A microorganism.

microorganism An organism that can only be seen with the aid of a microscope.

organism An individual living plant, animal, or microorganism.

outbreak A sudden rise in the occurrence of a disease in a particular area or population.

pandemic An outbreak of a disease that occurs over a large area.

phytoplankton Plankton composed of plants. Sea phytoplankton, which varies in amount depending on conditions such as light and temperature, is the main source of food, directly or indirectly, of all ocean organisms.

rehydrate To restore fluids to a dehydrated person.

sanitary Clean.

sanitation The act of making sanitary, or clean.

vaccine A preparation of living or dead microorganisms that is injected into an animal or human to produce or artificially increase immunity to a particular disease.

zooplankton Plankton composed of animals. These small floating or weakly swimming organisms drift with water currents in the ocean. Along with phytoplankton, zooplankton are the main source of food, directly or indirectly, for all ocean organisms.

For More Information

Interested in learning more about cholera? Check out these websites and organizations.

Websites

Brought to Life – Tracking Down the Source of Disease (Cholera)

www.sciencemuseum.org.uk/broughttolife/themes/publichealth/tracking_down.aspx

This website takes you on a journey through the streets of Soho, London. Follow John Snow as he tries to find the cause for the cholera outbreak affecting London's residents.

CDC Website on Cholera

www.cdc.gov/cholera/index.html

This page of CDC's website highlights any new information about cholera outbreaks and includes a map that identifies areas currently at risk.

The DOVE Project's Stop Cholera

www.stopcholera.org

This organization, DOVE (Deliver Oral Vaccine Effectively), looks to distribute the cholera vaccine to all at-risk populations.

Organizations

In the United States:

Centers for Disease Control (CDC)
1600 Clifton Road
Atlanta, GA 30333
(404) 639-3311; (800) 232-4636
Website: www.cdc.gov

The Pan American Health Organization
Regional Office of the World Health Organization
525 Twenty-third Street NW
Washington, DC 20037
(202) 974-3000
Website: www.paho.org

In Europe:

World Health Organization
Avenue Appia 20
1211 Geneva 27
Switzerland
Tel: (41 22) 791 21 11
Website: www.who.int

For Further Reading

Hamlin, Christopher. *Cholera: The Biography.* New York, NY: Oxford University Press, 2009.

Hempel, Sandra. *The Medical Detective: John Snow, Cholera, and the Mystery of the Broad Street Pump.* London, England: Granta Books, 2014.

Johnson, Steven. *The Ghost Map: The Story of London's Most Terrifying Epidemic—and How it Changed Science, Cities, and the Modern World.* New York, NY: Riverhead Trade, 2007.

Katz, Jonathan M. *The Big Truck That Went By: How the World Came to Save Haiti and Left Behind a Disaster.* New York, NY: Palgrave Macmillan, 2014.

Kotar, S. L. and J. E. Gesslar. *Cholera: A Worldwide History.* Jefferson, NC: McFarland & Company, 2014.

Parker, Steve. *Kill or Cure: An Illustrated History of Medicine.* New York, NY: DK Publishing, 2013.

Index

Index